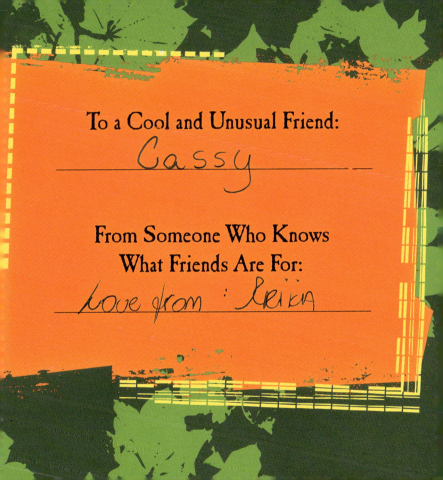

To a Cool and Unusual Friend:

Cassy

From Someone Who Knows What Friends Are For:

Love from: Erika

SHREK 2 ™

Are We FRIENDS Yet?

SHREK®

Andrews McMeel
Publishing

Kansas City

ARE WE FRIENDS YET?

Shrek is a registered trademark of DreamWorks L.L.C. Shrek 2™ & © 2004 DreamWorks L.L.C.
All rights reserved. Printed in Mexico.
No part of this book may be used or reproduced in any manner whatsoever without written
permission except in the case of reprints in the context of reviews.
For information, write Andrews McMeel Publishing, an Andrews McMeel Universal company,
4520 Main Street, Kansas City, Missouri 64111.

04 05 06 07 08 RR6 10 9 8 7 6 5 4 3 2 1

ISBN: 0-7407-4344-9

Library of Congress Control Number: 2003116331

Text by Cathy Hamilton

Book design by Holly Camerlinck

Attention: Schools and Businesses

Andrews McMeel books are available at quantity discounts with bulk purchase for educational,
business, or sales promotional use. For information, please write to: Special Sales Department,
Andrews McMeel Publishing, 4520 Main Street, Kansas City, Missouri 64111.

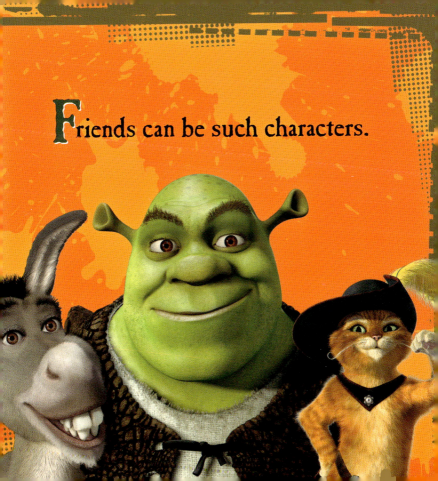

Some friends are adventurous and swashbuckling . . .

Some friends are sweet and charming . . .

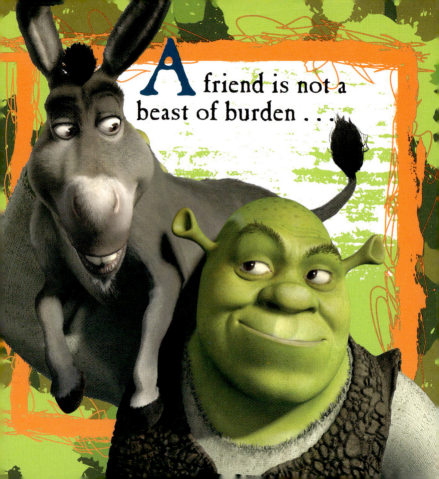

A friend is not a beast of burden . . .

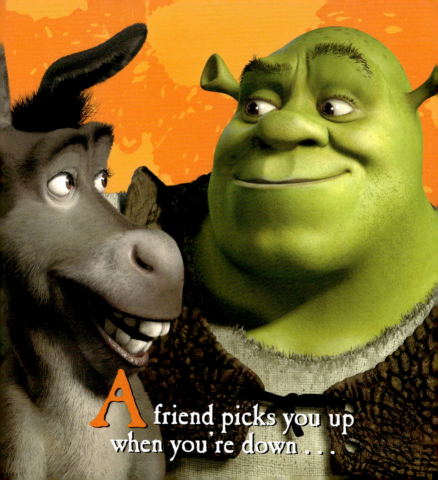

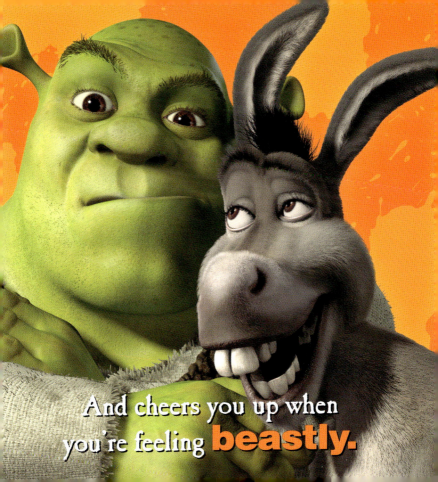

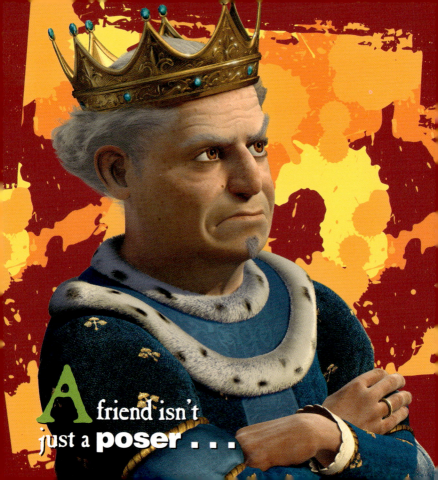

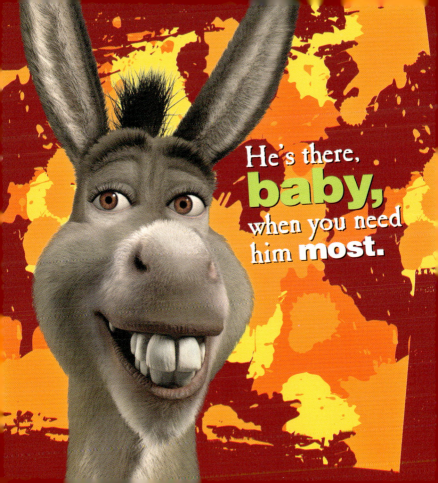

A friend likes your friends . . .

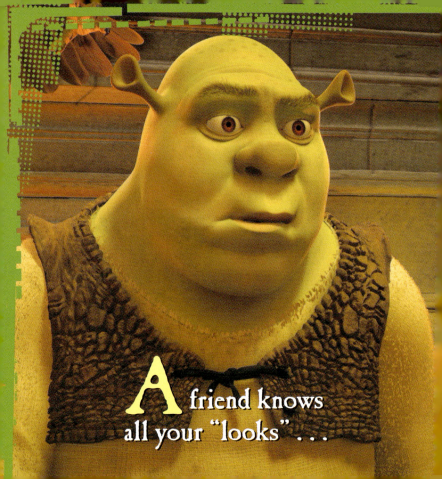

A friend knows all your "looks"...

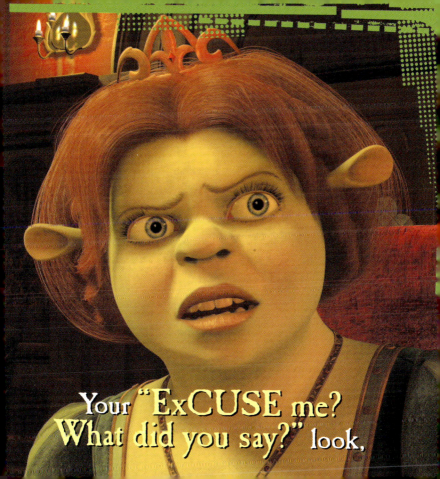

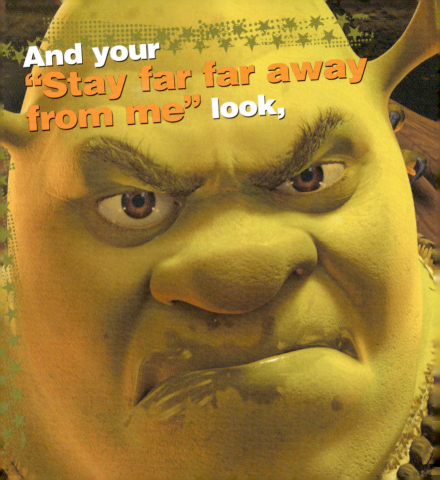

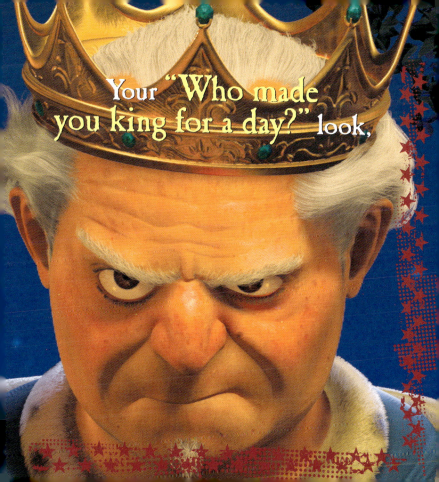

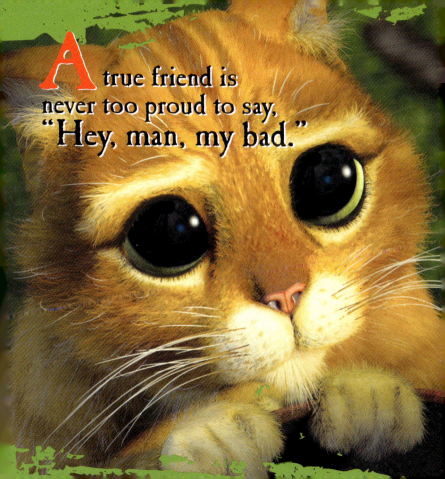

A true friend is never too proud to say, "Hey, man, my bad."

A friend is the first to say "Hey, good-looking . . ."

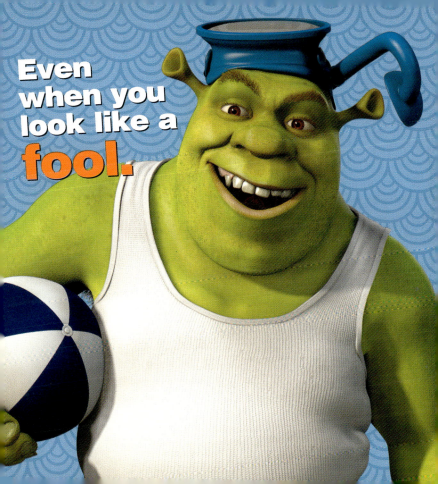

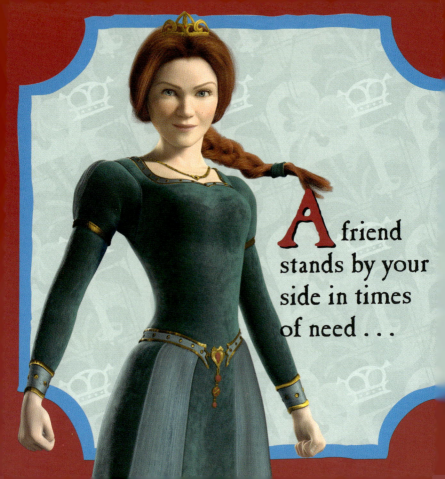

A friend stands by your side in times of need...

And **drop-kicks** your enemies into the next century.

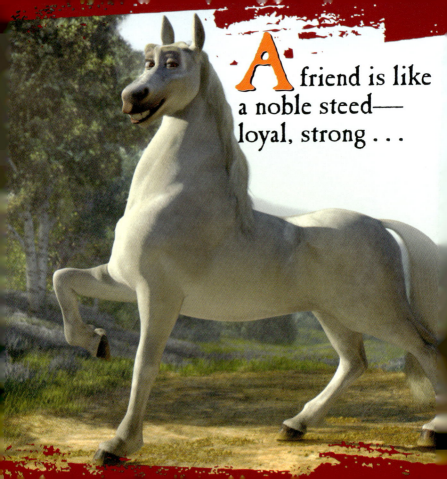

A friend is like a noble steed— loyal, strong . . .

And willing to go to bat for you.

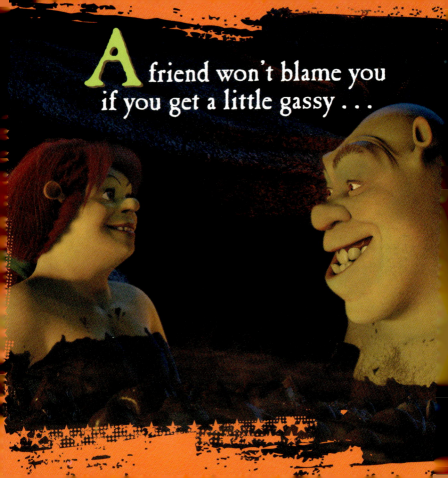

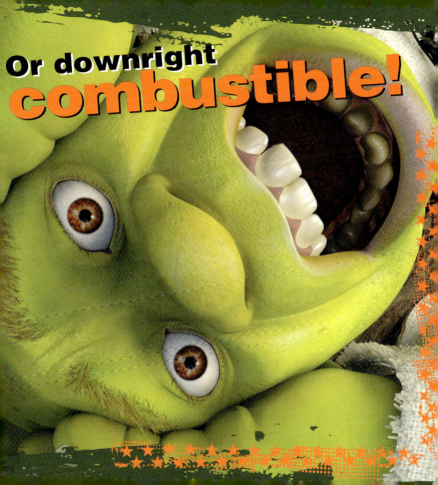

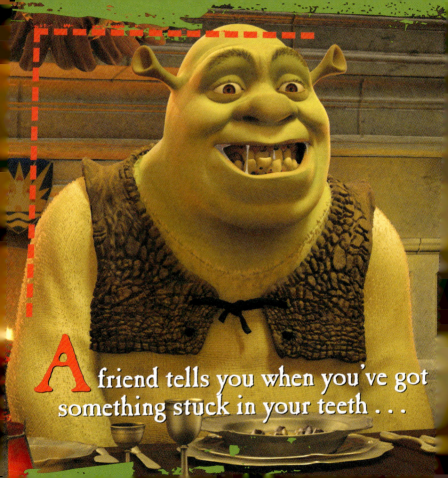

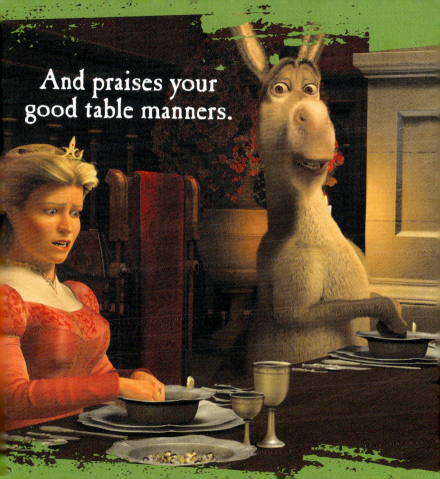

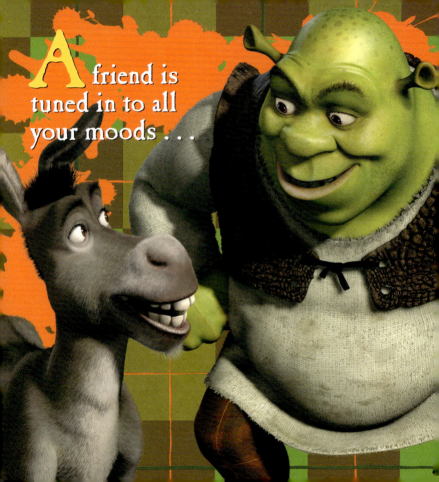

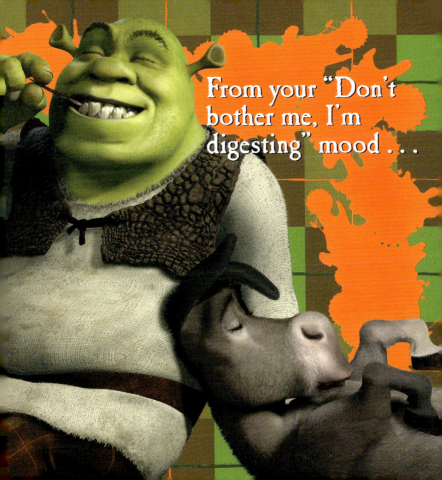

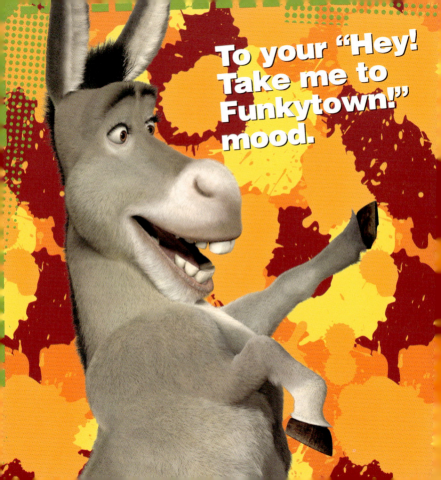

Friends don't worry when things go belly-up...

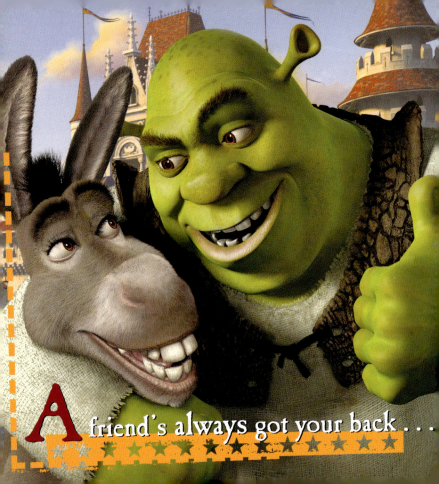

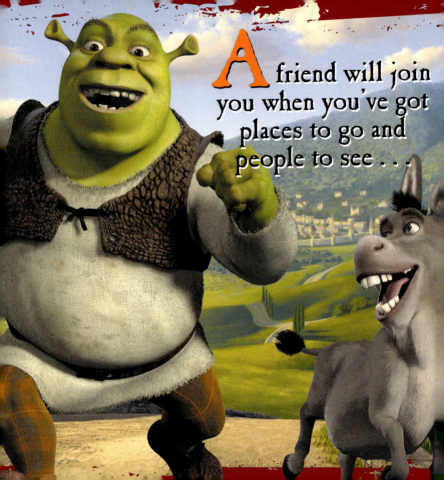

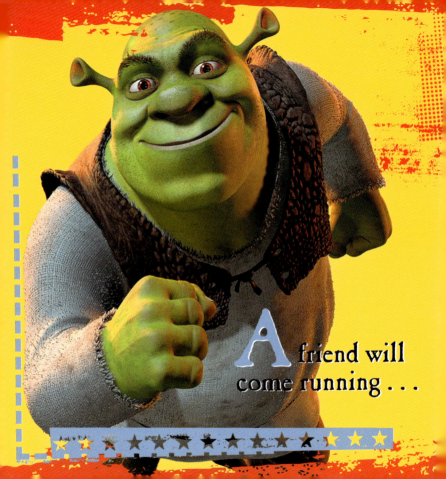

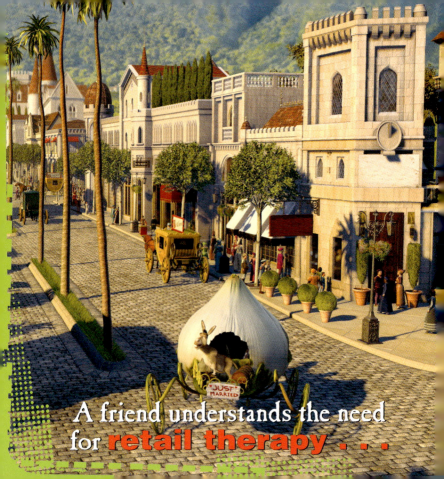

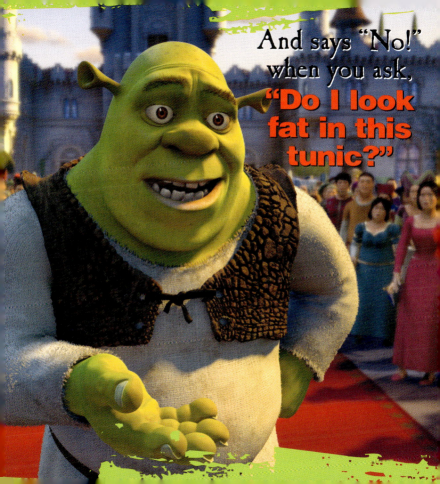

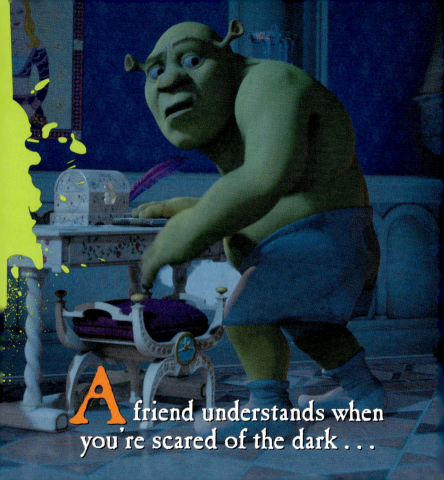

A friend understands when you're scared of the dark . . .